SWEEP HER OFF HER FEET:

Seriously, Dude, Clean Up Your Place!

By Jamie Reidy

Published 2018 by HumorOutcasts Press
Printed in the United States of America

ISBN: 0-9994127-6-0
EAN-13: 978-0-9994127-6-3

Cover art and design by:
Christine Georgiades
www.behance.net/georgie_psd

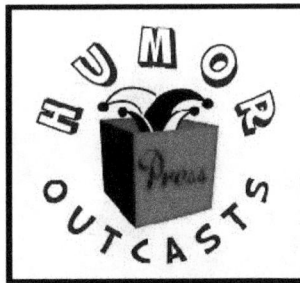

CONTENTS

INTRODUCTION

Consider You.

You remind me of me. Not that we've met or anything, but work with me, here.

You'd use your kitchen sink more often if you could only reach past the crusty dishes to get to the knobs. Your dust bunnies have multiplied into a cumulus cloud beneath your couch. Your fridge still contains pizza from three Super Bowl parties ago. Well, you're pretty sure it's pizza.

Take a look around your pad and ask yourself, "If I wanted to impress a woman tonight... what would I do differently?"

When I posed that question to myself, the answer bummed me out. *Uh, everything?* I had no idea I was such a slob! How I ever got a girl to make a return visit I do not know.

Sound familiar?

Objectively assessing my living space for the first time, I identified numerous problem areas and, thankfully, some easy ways to fix them. More importantly, I wrote them all down. Then, I asked eighty single women to email me their "deal breakers," things about a guy's apartment that would instantly repulse those ladies. You, you lucky dawg, will reap the benefits of their warnings. I even give you a checklist of the cleaning products necessary to get the apartment sparkling.

But I don't stop with the bachelor pad; I spell out ways to get the *bachelor* looking good, too. Just as a pilot goes through a Pre-flight checklist every time he flies, you need to examine yourself prior to every date. I have provided pre and post-shower routines to ensure you are ready for takeoff. Nose hairs? Backne? Brown weave belt? I've got you covered.

You want to look good enough that Ms. Right Now wants to drop her clothes in a heap on the floor. In order for that to happen, though, you gotta clean that floor!

ABODE

Getting Started

Pardon the vacuuming pun, but cleaning sucks. There's really no getting around that fact. You know the French Maid fantasy? I think half the turn-on is simply the hope that she might tidy up after the sex.

Here's a good way to approach cleaning, taken from that elder statesman of Modernism, Homer Simpson. In *The Simpson's* "Treehouse of Horror XI" episode, Homer's ghost is panicked that he won't be able to get into Heaven, so he asks Marge for suggestions on how best to do it.

> Marge: Well, I got a whole list of chores: clean the garage, paint the house...
>
> Homer's ghost: Whoa, whoa, whoa. I'm just trying to get in; I'm not running for Jesus!

Boys… we are also trying to get into Heaven, in a manner of speaking. And, like Marge says, chores are required.

Cleaning Essentials

- Vacuum

- Swiffer w/ Swiffer pads (This does a killer job of cleaning bare floors)

- Wet Swiffer w/ wet Swiffer pads (washes bare floors)

- Paper Towels

- Clorox Disinfecting Wipes

- Bathroom Cleaning Spray (Comet, Lysol, etc.)

- Glass Cleaner (Glass Plus, Windex, etc.)

- Q-Tips

- Brillo pads

- Old Sponge w/ green Astroturf side – 2

- Toilet Brush

- Toilet Brush Holder

- Baking Soda

- New Sponge w/ green Astroturf side

- Stick-Up air freshener

- Carpet Fresh

- Febreze Anti-microbial Fabric Freshener

On The Way In

Needs: Swiffer and dry Swiffer towels, or vacuum with hose attachment.

If you want Ms. Right Now to feel confident about walking inside, you need to clean outside.

Pick up and throw out all the ancient Pennysavers, unsolicited restaurant menus and "Have You Seen Me?" missing person postcards.

If Ms. Right Now must climb an indoor staircase en route to your place, you need to make sure the first thing she sees doesn't repulse her. In that spirit, it's a good idea to get rid of the cobwebs, pebbles, and dried mud that can accumulate on the riser (the vertical part that faces you) and in the corners of each step. On carpet or bare floor, you can use the vacuum with hose. The Swiffer (once you've attached a dry towel) only works on the bare floor.

The Swiffer is a contradiction in terms – a fun tool for cleaning. I don't understand the physics behind it, but somehow all the dirt and hair clings to the dry towel. All you have to do is move the Swiffer forward and back, left and right, like the optimist with the metal detector at the beach. (To maximize each towel, remove it from the device above the garbage can, so that the crap doesn't fall onto the floor; then, flip over the dry towel and use the clean bottom side, kinda like turning to the cool side of the pillow.)

Outside your apartment door. While not encouraging you to break any laws, it might behoove you to "temporarily" take down the Police Tape and the eviction notice.

Do you have a Welcome Mat? If so and it's less than two years old, that's good. If it's older, chuck that bad boy. You can buy a decent one at Target for $10. While you're looking down there – on the floor, not at Target – check for more dirt, etc. Swiffer/vacuum away whatever you find.

Once inside your apartment, make sure there is no footwear sitting by the door, especially not "aromatic" running shoes. Unless, that is, if you're operating with a "no shoes in the house" rule; then it's perfectly acceptable to have them neatly arranged door side. But not the running shoes!

Speaking of shoes, how long since you had yours shined? If time permits, drop them off at the local shoe shine guy; most full-service car washes have one. If you don't have the time, go get your shine box, Tommy. Or, at the very least, grab a wet paper towel and wipe down the pair you're going to wear on the date. Clean and dull is better than dirty and dull. My Opa – that's German for grandpa – always told me, "You can tell everything about a man by his shoes." What if her grandfather told her the same thing??? No need to risk it.

Harvard grads, since you already mentioned your alma mater within ten seconds of meeting her, anyway, you don't need to hang your diploma next to the coat rack.

Lastly, you need to recon your "spot." We've all got one – that special place where we drop our keys, wallet, phone, loose change, stripper's business cards, etc. Wherever it is, give your spot a thorough once-over. Who knows what is sitting out in plain sight for her to discover? Move any incriminating evidence to the *secret* location where you'll be storing your "sensitive" items.

__Kitchen__

Needs: New sponge with scrubbing side, Glass Plus, paper towels, Swiffer, Wet Swiffer, Arm & Hammer baking soda, cereal bowl, candles.

Did you know that the military acronym "K.P." stands for Kitchen Patrol?

Important rule of life: no matter how sweet the rest of the home, more people hang out in the kitchen during a party than in any other room. Same could be true on your date; especially if you are cooking for her or just grabbing beers from the fridge. Bottom line: you need to have the kitchen looking good, soldier.

When painting a room, you wouldn't do the walls before you did the ceiling, because that would cause specks of paint to splat down on the freshly done walls. You would start with the ceiling, and then do the walls. Cleaning a room is similar to painting – start high and work your way down.

Take a look in the four corners of the kitchen: see any arachnid apartments? They need to be razed. A big, scary spider is all right, as it'll provide you with the opportunity to heroically save the damsel in distress. Spider webs, however, only prove that you're harboring terrorists. And ISIS isn't getting laid.

Grab the vacuum hose, and suck down those webs.

Now, to the refrigerator.

Remove everything from the outside of the fridge and freezer doors. Soak the doors with Glass Plus, paying close attention to the area around the handles, just like in one of those TV commercials. Grab a couple of paper towels and wipe the doors down.

Take a deep breath… and rip open the refrigerator door. You are now in "Purge Mode."

Throw out anything you don't immediately remember buying, won't pass the whiff test or boasts condensation inside the bottle.

Unless you personally opened them yesterday, toss *all* jars of salsa.

Check the cold cuts and veggies drawers; you don't want her finding surprises later.

Now, carry those drawers over to the sink and scald them with the hottest water your faucet has to offer.

Wet the sponge. Wipe down all the shelves and racks in the fridge, making sure they are completely unstained.

Open the box of Arm & Hammer and place it in the back of the fridge. Yes, I do realize every Grandma in the world does this. That's because baking soda absorbs odors, sonny. Close the door.

Open the freezer door. Make sure there are no reminders of the warm can of Monster you put in there last fall "just for, like, ten minutes, only to get it cold." You know, the one you discovered a week later, exploded. If you find Slurpee parts, wipe them up with the sponge.

Empty out your ice tray in the sink, and be sure to depress the lever to make fresh ones. Yes, ice can go bad.

Here's an unrelated but fabulous rule for life: my Dad says you should always bring two bags of ice or two folding chairs to a party, because the host can never have too much of either. Everyone with whom I have shared that advice has scored major points after putting it into action. Rich Reidy –

the guy should've been on a Miller Lite "Man Law" commercial.

Ah, alcohol. Right now, drop everything!

Put the chardonnay, beer, tonic and club soda in the fridge and the vodka in the freezer. As long as the drinks are done correctly, you can atone for any meal mistakes.

If you are a frosted beer mug guy, make that happen.

If you want to make a classy impression, have a bottle of champagne chilling in the fridge at all times. You probably don't want to offer it right away – that might seem a bit much to her – but if things go well, she might like a taste of bubbly with/after dessert. And, even if you don't open it up, Ms. Right Now will see that you're a guy who always has champagne handy; nobody ever got demerits for that.

Back to the fridge doors.

Now that they're clean, you need to think about what you want decorating them. Just as the kitchen serves as the nucleus of the apartment, the refrigerator serves as the billboard of the kitchen.

She will make a beeline to read whatever is on your fridge, so be careful not to post anything negative – six parking tickets, angry statements from creditors, etc. Magnets from restaurants, sports teams and tourist locales are fine; magnets from bail bondsmen are not.

The easiest, safest and most effective way to spruce up your refrigerator is with kids' artwork. If any nieces or nephews live locally, call their mother and tell her you need some drawings addressed to "Uncle" ASAP. If time doesn't permit it, make a mental note to do so at the next earliest opportunity. Women appreciate a man who isn't too macho to display his love for children; what better way to do this than by displaying the terrible artwork of little people? It doesn't have to be drawn by relatives, though; any child will do. In fact, kids of friends may actually be better, thanks to the lack of a family obligation to hang it on the freezer.

From cold to hot: the microwave.

I'm guessing you haven't cleaned it since ever. First, fill up the cereal bowl with water, put it inside and cook it for a minute. The steam created will help loosen the splatter of a million nukings. Open the door carefully, so exploding water doesn't blind you, like in that Internet myth.

Grab the sponge and scrub like crazy. Take out the glass circle that spins in the middle and wash it in the sink. Don't forget to put it back after it's dry.

Scrub the inside of the door and wipe it down with a paper towel. Then, close said door and grab the Glass Plus. Spray the door and wipe it down with a paper towel.

Move over to the sink. Hopefully, you have a dishwasher, but most bachelors are not so lucky.

You gotta do the dishes and put them away in the cabinets *before* she arrives. Seriously. Throw the wine glasses in, too. I don't care if you think they're clean. They're not. Trust me: dust affects the bouquet. If you don't own wine glasses, you need to get some. Only four, and you can get them at Target, Williams Sonoma, or Crate and Barrel. (Note: the store's name is not Creighton Barrel, which is what I thought it was until I was 25.) Or borrow them from a female neighbor; this'll let that woman know you're not a total buffoon, which could pay off down the road.

Hold on. You're not done at the sink, yet.

If you have a dish rack for drying, you probably have one of those angled rubber mats, too. I can see the dirt and grime from here. Pick up the rack, and then rinse off and wipe down the rubber mat. Replace rack.

Sinks are often located in front of a window, making them great locations for a – gasp – plant. I'm not talking major shrubbery here, just one of those green, vine-like things that are impossible to kill.

Hang the plant from the ceiling. A single guy with living things in his home (not to be confused with mold, mice, ants, etc.) is a guy who's not totally terrified of one day entertaining the thought of *maybe* having children. She'll dig it.

On the topic of living creatures, obviously owning a dog is a huge plus in numerous areas. A cat accomplishes the same goals, while potentially adding an unwanted one: triggering her allergies.

Regardless, make sure that the food and water bowls are cleaner than everything in the house, including the wineglasses. Rover's bed shouldn't be covered with hair or smell like a dog sleeps there. Lastly, look for animal hair that has collected all along the baseboards. I will not even get into litter box maintenance.

Where's your trash?

Walk over there. If you do not have a *clearly designated* recyclables bin, you need to make one. Even a Recyclables Bag will do the trick. *Green…is good.* Women think eco-friendliness is hot. ABR – Always Be Recycling!

However, you should not have three 12-packs of empties inside the bin, lest she think you're a guy who sits around and pounds beers with his roomies on a Tuesday night while playing X-Box. (If you *are* that guy, that is totally fine. But she doesn't need to know you're that guy. Yet.)

Remember to actually use the recyclables bin later in front of her.

Just in case you'll be eating dinner, I'll cover how to set the table.

Obviously, you need to set two places. Across from one another is better for a date early in the relationship for two reasons: one, you won't freak her out with the creepy proximity; two, you get to make natural eye contact throughout dinner. If you're one of those guys who avoid eye contact, then, by all means, put the place settings on either side of the table corner.

Place a candle in the middle of the table. The dinner plate goes one inch from the table edge. The *fork* goes to the left of the plate, the *knife* to the right of the plate (blade inwards), and the *spoon* to the right of the knife. If you're serving salad, you need to do two extra things: place another fork next to his brother to the left of the plate and place the salad bowl on top of the plate.

The bread plate belongs on the upper left, while wine and water glasses go on the upper right. How do I know that last part?

Hold up each of your hands. Now, make the "O.K." sign with each. Your right hand looks like the letter "d" and your left looks like the letter "b", correct? D is for drinks and B is for bread. Drinks on the right, bread on the left. I learned that trick at a friend's bachelor party in Vegas. And to think my mom said nothing constructive happens on those weekends!

You should use cloth napkins (For real. You can get them at any of the aforementioned stores) but the nice paper kind will suffice. You don't need to use placemats. *Unless*, of course, the placemats have been made at kindergarten by your five-year old niece. Serve from the left side, clear the table from the right.

You probably haven't given any consideration to the chairs, but they're undoubtedly dusty: on top and between any spokes that run from the top to the base. Wipe off those areas. You'll be amazed how dirty the Clorox Disinfecting Wipe gets.

On to the kitchen floor. Why? Because if all goes well you might end up *on* the kitchen floor post-meal. Hey, if it happened to Jake Gyllenhaal in *Love and Other Drugs*, it can happen to you!

First, vacuum up all the crumbs, dirt, etc. Just to be safe, grab your Swiffer and catch any rogue hairs. Next, have fun with the wet Swiffer – the spray mechanism is a blast – and make that floor shine! Throw out the dirty pads for both Swiffers.

One last thing: hang a clean hand towel near the sink. After dinner, Ms. Right Now should – if her momma raised her right – offer to help do the dishes. This is a perfect time for some relaxed banter and lots of accidental touching.

Now, your kitchen looks and smells great. Nice work.

Living Room

Needs: Clorox Disinfecting Wipes, paper towels, candles, magazine rack, Glass Plus, vacuum, Swiffer, Wet Swiffer, Stick-Up air freshener, Carpet Fresh, Febreze Anti-microbial Fabric Freshener, one quarter (25-cent piece).

No pressure or anything, but this might be the most important room in the house. After all, you and she will probably be spending a lot of the date in here. No worries, mate; there are lots of easy fixes in the living room.

Again, start high. Grab the vacuum hose, and suck down those webs.

Next, look up at the ceiling fan, paying careful attention to the blades. See the layer of gray-brown fur hanging over the edges of each one? That isn't a strip of soundproofing that came with the fan.

Either climb on a chair and wipe down the blades with a Clorox Disinfecting Wipe, or use the vacuum's hose to clean them off.

Next, take a look at the "art work" adorning your walls. Neon beer signs are acceptable; beer posters with chicks in bikinis are not.

Got any framed photos of your family, or at least your mother? Better get some before your date starts thinking you're a serial killer. Several of the women I surveyed, however, cautioned against having *too many* pictures of Mom – they make you look like a mama's boy and indicate the presence of a smothering future mother-in-law.

Shots of a family pet are guaranteed to induce an "Awww." Pictures of your ex do not. The women surveyed also complained about those annoying framed prints that your boss has on the wall of his office, the ones with the cheesy inspirational messages. So you might want to 86 any of those.

Take the Clorox Disinfecting Wipes and wipe down the tops and edges of anything hanging on the walls.

If you just wiped down a gun rack with actual guns in it... that's probably a deal breaker in Blue States. Even in a Red State, unless you know for sure that you're dating a direct descendant of Annie Oakley, she may spot your arsenal, click her spurs three times and disappear before you refill her wine glass. Consider yourself warned, Tex. Ditto for antlers or anything that ever required a conversation with a taxidermist.

Speaking of spooking her, reptiles are not conducive to getting naked. This is not up for discussion. If you own a parrot or any other winged creature, make sure to cover that cage, Bird Boy.

Next, take a Clorox Disinfecting Wipe and wipe it along the edges of your halogen lamps (c'mon, everybody's got at least one). Try not to cough on the dust you've kicked up.

Next, move to the bookcase. (I hope to God I'm not going out on a limb, here, by assuming that you own books.) Give the shelves a quick wipe down.

If you have any books that were published since you did your required summer reading in high school, put those on a shelf that's right at your gal's line of sight. "I Know This Much Is True" and "Fault in Our Stars" will demonstrate your sensitive side, while anything by Malcolm Gladwell will let her know you're hip to smart non-fiction.

Several respondents specifically listed "The Kama Sutra" as a book that should not be on a bookshelf. Apparently, women want us to *read* it, but they don't want to *see* it.

If you have a Fat Head of the Bud Girl or Kendall Jenner or any other woman, please consider hiding it in your buddy's apartment down the hall or stashing it in the way back of the closet. As for male Fat Heads, my friend Denis grew up adoring Dan Marino, the Miami Dolphins' Hall of Fame quarterback. All throughout his twenties, he – Denis, not Dan – had a life-sized cutout of #13 in uniform standing guard in his TV room. Amazingly, he got married seventeen years ago. Even more amazing, Denis still has Dan The Man standing guard in his TV room *and* is still married.

Regardless, I do not recommend such risk taking.

On to your pride and joy: your TV.

Dampen a cloth or paper towel and gently wipe down the TV. Same with the cable box and the DVD player, if you have them.

Take a seat, for a second. You earned it! Okay, that's enough.

Speaking of the couch, pull off all the cushions. This is more than a task designed to find you enough change to pay for a Spicy Tostada at Taco Bell; this is a preemptive strike.

Let's say things are going well – really well – and you and Ms. Right Now end up rolling around on the couch. In the heat of the moment, she sticks out a hand to brace herself, but it slips between the cushions… and she ends up with Frito crumbs stuck to her palm. I can practically hear the sound of Yoda dying.

Grab the vacuum hose, and clean up the exposed couch. Replace the pillows and prop them up all nice-like. Then, grab the Febreze and lightly mist the cushions; not that I think your couch might need some anti-microbials or anything.

If you're a future lung cancer patient, I mean, Smoker, move every ashtray to the deck or fire escape. I know, I know: it's *your* castle and you can do whatever you want inside it. With that attitude, Prince Charming, you're not making out tonight or any time soon. Statistics say your princess will not appreciate a pile of butts stinking up the joint. Move 'em.

If you're a future lip cancer patient, I mean, Dipper, scour the apartment for the six forgotten beer bottles half-filled with your brown spit. Recycle those Skoal Cocktails, and immediately take the trash outside before you have a Category 3 Haz Mat situation on your hands.

Your bong. If you already know she has a cannabis card, it probably doesn't matter where you keep it. If you don't know, play it safe and stick it in the closet. You can always pull out the vaporizer after the topic comes up.

Cocaine-dusted mirrors or heroin kits, however, should probably remain hidden until she says something like, "Who do I have to blow around here to get a fix?"

I'm not sure where you maintain your home office so I'll just address this important area now.

You don't have to clear your desktop of mail, random papers, etc.

But you do need to put them in some kind of order, indicating that you actually have "a system." Even if you and I know you kinda don't.

Most importantly, you don't want to leave visible any "Past Due" utility bills or $30,000 Visa balances. Ditto for restraining orders.

On the flip side, if you have a big fat pay stub you wouldn't mind her seeing, you might leave it "half hidden" on the desk; after all, the medicine cabinet isn't the only place she might snoop.

If you like to leave your laptop open, delete all recent history that you wouldn't want your mom to see.

As a final desk requirement, use the Clorox Disinfecting Wipes to wipe down the lamp, stapler, paper clip dispenser, etc.

On to the coffee table. I don't know exactly what's on top, but I know it's covered with crap. Take it all off. Something tells me you may have forgotten what color it was. Am I right?

Grab the Glass Plus and spray the top of the table, or whatever semi-flat object you've been using as a coffee table. Wipe it down with a paper towel. There may be some "stuff" on there that takes repeated sprayings and scrubbings.

Grab two candles and place them strategically around the living room. You don't often get to freelance, Private, so take advantage of the opportunity.

Dude, you are *so* almost done. Only floor duty remains.

If you have a hardwood floor, follow the same steps as in the kitchen: vacuum, Swiffer, Wet Swiffer. Be careful not to Wet Swiff yourself into a corner.

If you have carpeting, fire up that vacuum. Rug guys, if you've had a party in the past two months, you might want to sprinkle some Carpet Fresh and re-vacuum. Not that anybody would ever spill a beer at a soiree of yours. Actually, you know what? Let's not limit that instruction to party throwers. *Everybody*, sprinkle the Carpet Fresh and re-vacuum.

Drop a quarter on the floor. Watch it roll. Get down on all fours to pick it up. (It doesn't *have to be* a 25-cent coin, but that'll be easier to find.)

While you're down there, take a look around: you might see something under the couch or TV stand or desk you missed earlier. Try the quarter thing a few more times; you'll be glad you did.

Make one last sweep of the living room, keeping a vigilant eye out for dirty paper towels and Swiffer cloths.

Admire your handiwork. But don't sit down!

<u>Bathroom</u>

Needs: Glass Plus, Comet Bathroom Cleaner, Drano, Swiffer, Wet Swiffer, Swiffer pads both dry and wet, vacuum, old dishwashing sponge with Astroturf side, Q-tips, Clorox Disinfecting Wipes, paper towels, two new tooth brushes, toilet brush <u>and</u> toilet brush holder.

Before you do anything, open the window and hit the exhaust fan; you'll be using enough cleaning agents to sedate a kindergarten.

Once again, start at the top.

Grab the vacuum with the hose attachment. Look up at the corners. See any cobwebs? Perhaps not. This may be due to the fact that the upper walls are covered by one continuous web. Suck it away, sir!

Don't put down the vacuum hose just yet.

Turn off the bathroom fan, which, in my estimation, is the third greatest home invention of the past 50 years, trailing only the TV remote and WiFi. Take a good look at the grate covering the fan. It's all gunked up, isn't it? Use the vacuum hose to free your friend from its dust shackles and let the fan do the job it was born to do.

Ever see that Southwest Airlines commercial where the woman opens the guy's medicine cabinet and all the glass shelves fall out, totally busting her? (It's worth the Google.) Everyone laughs at that one because it's true; chicks are Super Snoopers. Rather than try to reverse millions of years of DNA encoding, just deal with it.

Open said medicine cabinet. Clear off the shelves. Grab a few Clorox Disinfecting Wipes and wipe them down. Next, wipe down everything that was on those shelves (saline solution cases, in particular, attract grime). Return everything to its rightful spot.

Uh, you might want to put the following items – in descending order of importance – someplace a little less public: Valtrex, Lithium, Viagra, Propecia, PreparationH, Compound W, and Beano.

You may want to leave your Xanax in there, since some ladies like a lad who has been to therapy. That's your call.

Speaking of Viagra, if you're still using Vitamin V instead of Cialis, you're missing out. And I say that as an original member of Pfizer's Urology sales force that launched Viagra. A 36-hour "window of opportunity" beats the crap out of a 4-hour window. And since you're stealing the samples from your father's/uncle's/friend's medical practice, anyway, why not participate in a modern day Pepsi Challenge? See if you can tell the difference. You won't be disappointed.

Back to the medicine cabinet! Make sure you move your dental floss, toothpaste, and ACT plaque rinse to the first shelf, right at *female* eye level! Dental hygiene seems to be way more important to women than it is to men.

Close the medicine cabinet. Look in the mirror.

If your reflection is obscured by more than zero self-motivational Post-It notes, remove each and every one of them immediately. Good God, are you insane, man? That's like hanging little, "Here are the areas where I am most vulnerable and can be taken advantage of with the least effort!" signs. (Note: If you have any of these on the dashboard of your car, run outside and get rid of those, too.)

Look in the mirror again.

You probably don't see yourself very clearly. This is reminiscent of Joe Pesci's title character in *My Cousin Vinny*, when he's cross-examining a witness. Vinny points to an evidentiary photo of a window screen, and asks, "What's all this… *stuff*?" After a moment the redneck witness hesitantly replies, "Dirt?" Vinny smiles reassuringly and says, "That's right! Don't be afraid. Go ahead and shout it out!"

So, you're staring at your mirror and you're thinking it's fairly clean. *Dude.* The girl who's coming over tonight could teach a CSI team a thing or two about finding incriminating evidence. She can tell when you switched from Colgate to Crest, and that you had an infected whitehead last month.

Grab the Glass Plus and drench that glass. Dry it with a paper towel in a consistent up and down motion.

Now, look down at the sink. Unfortunately, apartments often have poor drainage, allowing generations of dripped-off toothpaste and shaved whiskers to create barnacles in your sink. I understand this and share your belief that there's no use in cleaning them off each time because their cousins will stick there eventually. Alas, Ms. Right Now does not agree with you and me.

Turn on the hot water and, once it's scalding, plug the drain. When the sink is full, turn off the water and let the water sit like that for a few minutes, hopefully softening up the crust.

Do ten pushups. What, you don't want to be pumped up for your date?

Back to the sink. Unplug the drain. Drown the sink in Comet Bathroom Cleaner. Let it soak in for a moment.

Then, with Astroturf sponge in hand, start scrubbing as feverishly as you'd clean up the blood from a crime scene. Just saying.

If you have sink drainage issues, read this. If not, skip to the next paragraph. Grab the Drano and pour half the bottle down the sink. It needs to sit for 15 minutes.

Once the sink shines like the day you moved in, raise your line of sight to the basin (that's the area around the sink).

Remove your razor, shaving cream, toothpaste, etc. Spray the surface with Comet Bathroom Cleaner. Let that soak in before wiping the basin down.

Next, take your Glass Plus and drench the fixtures. Let the liquid soak in. Wiping these down will take some serious elbow grease, as they probably haven't been cleaned since Deadpool started cracking wise while offing dudes.

Once that's done, lean toward the wall and peer down into the tiny gap between the faucet and the back of the basin. *Ick*. Grab a Q-tip and try to clean up as much of that gunk as possible. Do this with several different Q-tips.

Now, as with the medicine cabinet, you need to wipe down every object that was on the basin, paying particular attention to the crud on your razor holder and the dust on top of your shaving cream can top. (If you use an electric razor to trim your goatee or, like me, use clippers to cut what hair you have left, make sure you look carefully for whiskers that have floated onto weird spots: the wall, the window sill, etc.)

The need to remove the shaving cream, razor and toothpaste reminds me of a painful lesson. After receiving a sudden job promotion to California, I put my home in Indiana up for sale and left it in the questionable hands of my two roommates. Despite a large number of showings, the realtor could not sell the house, jeopardizing the 2% of the sale price bonus I would have received from Pfizer as reward for saving the company the hassle of buying the house as part of my relocation deal. After one annoyed voice mail from the realtor mentioned, "The smell of wet dog," I decided to place a call to my roomies back in Indiana.

Steve shared a conversation he'd had with his then girlfriend, now wife, Michelle. Exiting the bathroom shortly after prospective buyers had toured the house, she asked Steve, "So, you take your shaving cream and razor off the basin for the showing, and then put it back right after they leave?" Steve's clueless look said it all: he never once put away the toiletries before any of the showings. Pfizer had to buy my house and I never did collect that 2% bonus.

Think of women as prospective homebuyers; they're not pulling the trigger when a can of Edge is rusting up the basin. Do yourself a favor, and store that stuff in the medicine cabinet, or build a shelf.

Take a step back from the sink and look down at the other oval object in the bathroom. Yes, I hear the lambs still screaming, too.

The toilet. Ugh.

Let's start off easy: Toilet paper. I don't care what brand you have or what thickness it is (though I am a two-ply man, myself). Just make sure you have enough of it. Remember, women use TP *every time* they go. Every time. You're gonna need a back up roll, brother. Also, spend the extra ten seconds it takes to place the roll on the actual toilet paper dispenser. This, by itself, will distinguish you from 90% of the guys she ever dated.

Remove everything from the top of the toilet tank. Wipe it down with a Clorox Disinfecting Wipe.

Pick up the five books of matches you have handy to override the occasional odoriferous offense, and throw out any you obtained from a Gentleman's Club. Take the G-rated ones and place them in a nice, little bowl. (Women love their little bowls.) In fact, it's a good idea to buy a matching set of bathroom items (soft soap dispenser, waste basket, little bowl and toothbrush holder) at Target or Bed, Bath and Beyond. Trust me, she won't think you're gay. But if you don't have time for that two-hour adventure to the store, simply find a bowl or glass jar to hold the matches as a stopgap measure.

With that lay-up under your belt, you're graduating to the tougher challenges. It might not be a bad idea to take a page out of Michael Keaton's handbook from *Mr. Mom* and place a clothespin over your nose.

For a good example of how to properly clean a toilet (and to continue this string of cinematic cleaning references), rent *Singles*, writer/director Cameron Crowe's legendary homage to the Grunge Era in Seattle. Pay close attention to Kyra Sedgwick's technique using her ex-boyfriend's T-shirt as a tool.

Bottom line: you gotta get down on your knees and scrub all the unintended targets you and your buddies have undoubtedly strafed with friendly fire.

Focus carefully on the run-off channels down the sides and the area beyond the "center field wall," as I like to call it.

Empty a few rounds of Comet into the toilet. You'll come back to this in a minute.

Take a Clorox Disinfecting Wipe or paper towel and wipe down the dusty underside of the toilet lid.

Next, lift up the toilet seat. See those brown stains? The Space Shuttle makes less of a splash upon reentry than you do the day after a 3:00AM burrito.

Drench that bad boy in Comet Bathroom Cleaner and let it soak in. Saturate your old dishwashing sponge in the sink.

Now, grab your toilet brush and go to town on the toilet bowl. Be aggressive, as if you're grilling out and just dropped a $30 N.Y. strip into the coals. Concentrate on the narrow bottom of the bowl, and don't forget to jam the brush under the lip where the water comes out; "stuff" sometimes hides there.

Flush. It's easy to check your progress: lighter colored areas are better than darker areas. Keep scrubbing and flushing until the entire bowl is uniform in color (uniformly "yellowish" is not acceptable unless the top of the toilet tank is yellowish).

Rinse off the brush by sticking it under the clean water after a flush. Repeat. Now, shake it off above the toilet before replacing it in its holster.

Back to the underside of the toilet seat, the cleaning equivalent of a hockey defenseman's diving in front of a slap shot. Grab the wet sponge and flip it over so that the Astroturf side is the active one. Start scrubbing.

Once you've eradicated the incriminating evidence, wipe the bottom (no pun intended) and top of the seat with Clorox Disinfecting Wipes. Then, toss them and the sponge into the HazMat bin behind your place.

You should practice always putting down the toilet seat in your own home. This way, it will become second nature to you, eliminating the risk of leaving the seat up at her place and proving you are a selfish ogre.

My cousin Brian (a former US Army Ranger), however, recommends the opposite course of action if you ever have to take a dump at one of those bars with the trendy unisex bathrooms.

Obviously, drop the deuce as fast as possible. Afterwards, though, leave the seat in the upright *position. If you exit to find a gal waiting next in line, immediately make a pained expression to assure her that it was the guy in front of you who destroyed the place.*

She won't believe you – smart girl – but ten seconds later when she sees the toilet seat in the upright position, she will realize that since you never sat down, you couldn't be the poop perp.

And you'll still have a chance to cook for her the next weekend.

Morning After note: Once you've awoken and taken your Austin Powers piss, grab some toilet paper and wipe up the floor in front of the toilet where her bare feet will rest when she uses the facilities. Splashing around in your urine first thing in the morning will not rev her engines for another lap around your bed.

Back to the now.

Turn on the hot water in the sink. Let it run for a minute, rinsing the Drano away.

At this point, you deserve a break. Grab a quick drink of water, flip on the TV to check out some scores, but whatever you do… don't sit down!

To paraphrase Vince Lombardi, "Cleaning the bathroom makes cowards of us all." It's way too easy to stay seated once you've schlumped down on your couch. Rally and stay focused. You need to finish what you've started – do the job right, President George Herbert Bush, and steamroll all the way into Baghdad!

Need motivation?

Visualize her standing in your bathroom. The mirror shines, the sink gleams, the toilet sparkles. *Hmm, this guy cleans! I may need to shower with him later.* But the shower has to dazzle her before she puts Operation Soapy Soapy into motion.

You'll begin *outside* the shower.

I'm assuming you only own one bathmat. And you've had it since graduation. And you've never even dreamed of washing it because your wet feet wash it every morning. I'm also assuming that you do not have time to wash that old friend before she arrives.

Pick up the mat and fold it inward like you're a hobo who's about to tie it to a stick before hopping a freight train. Take the bathmat out back behind your place and – after closing your eyes and taking a deep breath – start shaking it out. Rest. Breathe. Repeat. Now, furiously brush off the dust and pubes that have settled into your hair and onto your shirt.

This is a good time for me to recommend purchasing a bath rug, or something more substantial than the glorified washcloths found in your old dorm's shower room. Preferably, this bathmat will match your collection of bath towels, which, in turn, will match the bathroom's color scheme. (Yeah, you definitely need to schedule a trip to Bed, Bath and Beyond, preferably chaperoned by a sister or gal pal.)

When it comes to towels, women think bigger is better. Investing in two "bath sheets" – the ones that can wrap her up several times over – is a good move.

Don't forget that girls use washcloths and those mini-towels that don't really have any purpose. Make sure you have those ready for sleepovers. Yes, those have to match, too. At an absolute minimum, they cannot have "Motel 6" printed on them.

Oh, yeah. I almost forgot. All the towels you put out MUST be clean.

Do not hang your shower towel near the shitter!!! Cloth absorbs odors; wet cloth traps them. Nothing like drying off with a towel emitting a whiff of the aforementioned damage from that 3 AM burrito.

Back to the decontamination.

I'm guessing that your shower curtain isn't fit to wrap a dead body in, let alone hang in your bathroom. If time is not an issue, pull it down, roll it up and throw it in the rapidly filling Hazmat bin. Then go buy a new one at Target or BBB. (Remember, it should jibe with the color concept you've got going. Also, clear shower curtains allow more light in through the window, which could be a good thing or bad thing depending on the age and quality of your bathroom. I once had a clear curtain with yellow duckies on it; big hit with the ladies.)

If you don't have time for the shopping mission, step inside the shower and drench the curtain with Comet Bathroom Cleaner; at least that might kill some living organisms.

For those of you with glass shower doors, you gotta get one of those squeegee things and use it with Glass Plus. Seriously.

Remove everything from the shower. Liquid-wise, this should only include a bottle of shampoo, a bottle of conditioner, and a bottle of body wash, a.k.a. liquid soap.

Any exfoliating creams, tightening lotions, etc. should be hidden. You don't want to have more stuff than she does, Guy. Tool-wise, you can have a scrub brush and a washcloth – that's it. If you have one of those nylon thingies that looks like a jellyfish, I'd hide it. But, that's me.

Like with everything else, start at the highest point and work your way down.

Take a look at the showerhead. If you see anything other than air in the holes, you need to blast it with cleaner and scrub like crazy. Hello, mold.

Stand back and stare at your shower walls. See any dark spots? Dude, you've been hosting a botany experiment, and you didn't even know it. Chicks can sense mold spots with the lights turned off, like a disturbance in The Force. Fortunately, correcting your mold problem is easy. Sadly, it takes a lot of elbow grease. Douse the walls with Comet cleaner, and let it soak in for a few minutes. Do some arm stretches. Then, grab your sponge and start scrubbing.

Regardless of whether you store the bar of soap in the built-in wall slot or on a rack hanging from the showerhead, you will need to clean the soap dish. For real. How many dead soldiers do you have piled up like melted candles? I'm guessing at least three. While I respect your adherence to military code – "Never leave your dead!" – Ms. Right Now will definitely not appreciate the art project gone bad.

Scrape off the lumpy, hard ball of soap and throw it out. Next, scrub the dish, so no remnants remain. Do the same thing to the trail of soap that has dripped down the wall and hardened. (Also, when you have an overnight guest, you will be expected to provide a *new* bar of soap, one that is still in the box. My ex-girlfriend insisted on doing that, claiming that nobody wanted to use the same bar of soap I'd been using. I fought her on it – and lost – but I must grudgingly admit now that she was right. *Probably woulda helped to figure that out two years ago, genius!* Okay, and that concludes Jamie's Therapy Session.)

Back in the shower. Look down at your feet. Try not to cry. Probably not necessary for me to tell you what to do, but just to be sure: get down on your knees and start scrubbing.

(Note: one of those rubber, no-slip mats is a great way to cover up a dirty shower floor. Plus, she'll think safety's important to you. "Safety" could trigger thoughts of "safe sex," which may lead to her thinking, "I hope he has condoms!" However, a dirty rubber mat may be grosser than the dirty tub floor the former is supposed to hide, which would defeat the purpose entirely. You will definitely score points with one of those wooden platforms with the slats, but they cost a lot more.)

The drip area below the faucet is undoubtedly discolored, probably indelibly from hard water; but since you're already down on your knees, give it a good scrub. For the team.

In that same area of operation, examine the drain. *Psst.* It's underneath the pound of matted pubes, chest hair and hair hair. Might wanna remove that human Brillo pad.

If your tub/shower has drainage problems, do yourself a favor and pre-emptively use the rest of the Drano. Standing ankle deep in scummy water is not going to entice your angel to invite you in for the aforementioned soapy soapy.

Now, run the hot water and wash down every surface in the shower.

"They're coming down the homestretch..."

To the bathroom floor. Fellas, we are hairy bastards. First vacuum and then keep Swiffing until the floor no longer resembles a barbershop at closing time. Next, wet Swiffer. Take the used Swiffer pads out to the Haz Mat bin.

Your last chore will be done under the assumption that your efforts will be rewarded.

If Ms. Right Now spends the night, she will more than likely want to brush her teeth – especially in the morning. But she likely didn't pack a toothbrush in her purse. If you have a case of toothbrushes at her disposal, though, she might think you're a bit *too prepared* for sleepovers. Since dentists recommend replacing your toothbrush every three months, having one or two on hand isn't a sign of promiscuity, but oral sensibility.

Place the new toothbrushes in the medicine cabinet or in a bin under the sink.

Now, look in that gleaming mirror and smile. I know this is a lot to remember, but never forgot the old cliché: confidence is key. As Andy Dwyer from *Parks and Recreation* once said, "I have no idea what I'm doing, but I know I'm doing it really, really well."

Bedroom

Needs: Vacuum cleaner with hose attachment, Glass Plus, paper towels, clean sheets, candle, Kleenex, clothes hamper.

The bedroom is like the Red Zone in a football game, isn't it? The Steelers spend all this money (on players), time (strategizing) and energy (training and practicing) to score inside the 20-yard line.

Team You spends all this money (on food and beverages), time (acquiring the necessities) and energy (cleaning) to score in the bedroom.

As usual, you're starting high and working your way down. Cobweb duty all around the room. Those with a ceiling fan, you know what to do.

If you have mirrors on the ceiling, I salute you, sir! And I suggest you come up with an acceptable explanation for their presence in your home.

If you live in one of those apartment complexes in which every bedroom is festooned with mirrored closet doors, you don't need an explanation. You do, however, need to make sure they are free of any fingerprints and "smudges."

Grab the Glass Plus and a paper towel and get to work.

Take a gander at your walls. Just like in the living room, beer posters are not allowed, but *neither are* neon beer signs. This is a sacred space, for crying out loud. If you're looking to buy something to hang on the wall, women like framed prints of French lighthouses, French train stations, French paintings, and French bulldogs.

Wipe everything down with paper towels and Glass Plus.

Remove everything from the top of your dresser. *You use milk crates to store your clothes?* If you are under 25, that is permissible. If older than 25, they've invented this place called Ikea. Go there. Immediately.

Wipe off the top of the dresser.

You're not done with the Glass Plus or paper towels. Move over to your nightstand – you do have a nightstand, right? If not, add that to your IKEA list.

Remove everything from the nightstand. Spray down that dusty top and wipe it clean. Now, wipe the lamp off and put it back in place. Dust off the lampshade. If you still have a clock, wipe it down and put it back where it belongs.

Grab the candle and place it on the nightstand's outside corner where the flame will be maximized. Now, light it. You will blow it out in a bit; after all, you don't want it to burn so much that it appears you've had a hundred girls sleep over, but you also don't want the wick looking brand new, as if you just busted out the candle today to try and impress her. Even though you totally did.

Now, place a book on the table. *Which* book isn't important, but the fact that it is being read *is*. For a hardcover, open it, take out the front jacket flap, and place it between two random pages; with a paperback, do the same random move and fold the page in half lengthwise.

It'd be smart to actually read the pages to which you've opened the book, just in case she administers a Pop Quiz. Teacher always did like the kids who were prepared!

A picture of your family or a non-vulgar one of your buddies is a nice touch.

There's just one thing left to add to the nightstand. Let's say Ms. Right sneezes during the night. What are you going to hand her to soak up the snot at that increasingly awkward moment? Toilet paper ain't gonna cut it.

Open the Kleenex box and place it on top, if there's room, or underneath if there isn't.

Blow out the candle.

If you have a TV in your bedroom, repeat the cleaning steps from the living room.

Finally, you've reached the Promised Land: your bed. Don't fumble on the goal line!

This is a good time to mention that several women surveyed had major problems with men who still own stuffed animals. Something to think about.

When a visitor walks into a bedroom, the first thing she naturally looks at is the bed. This fact elevates the comforter's status to: most important object in the room. Have you ever seen an unattractive hostess at a hip restaurant? Didn't think so. Your comforter, like a hostess, represents the entire organization.

With that possibly frightening thought in mind, I've got a mental exercise for you consisting of two questions: how old you were when you got that comforter, and who paid for it?

If the answers are "Five or more years younger than I am now" and/or "Mom," it's probably time for a new comforter. If *you* bought it *less* than five years ago, but it has those fuzzy fabric balls sticking to it, it's probably time for a new comforter. (The fuzzy fabric balls are known as "pilling," btw.)

If you don't have time to run to Bed, Bath and Beyond before Ms. Right Now arrives, though, add this to your to-buy list and drop your comforter off at the dry cleaner's. If you don't even have enough time for that, hang it outside for 30 minutes. If hanging it outside is not an option, spray the comforter with a dash of Febreze and then flip it over to its less fabric ball-y side.

Lift off the comforter; take a good look at the sheets. Think for a moment. If you did not just put them on the bed yesterday, immediately rip them off.

Clean sheets are an absolute must! But comfort is important, too. The higher the thread counts, the better off you are.

Thread count is the number of horizontal and vertical threads in one square inch of fabric, and the number can range from 80 to 700. Most stores sell sheets that range from 180 to 320. In general, the higher the thread count, the softer the fabric will feel on her skin. For your purposes, anything over 300 will be rewarded.

I'm guessing you or your mother bought your pillows along with the comforter. People are quite particular about their pillows, so I'm not going to advise you on fluffy, firm, etc. I will say that comparisons to sleep-away camp pillows are not a good thing.

Remember to throw the pillowcases into the washing machine with the sheets when you do laundry. But not the pillows.

Having remade the bed, go get the quarter you used in the living room. Walk back into the bedroom and drop the coin. Take a long look underneath the bed and dresser.

Anything there you don't want her to see, like used Kleenex, empty condom wrappers, or an ex's thong?

Remove any evidence you discover. Obviously, your "crusty" towel will have to be relocated for the evening.

Stand up and look all around the floor. See any wayward jeans or T-shirts?

In a pinch you can always use the traditional last resort of throwing all the dirty clothes into the closet, but that's risky. What if our super snooper expands her search parameters outside the medicine cabinet and desk?

You really need some type of receptacle in which to place your laundry. Whether it's a $40 tri-plex from Target that lets you isolate the clothes by colors, or simply two plastic wash-baskets you'll be okay. (Why two wash-baskets? Because it's important to show her you know that darks don't go with lights, so you need more than one hamper-like thing.)

If you wear thongs or Manties, bury them at the bottom of the pile.

Having picked up your clothes from the floor, take a look at that flat space you probably haven't seen in a while.

You should know the drill by now: Swiffer for hardwood, or the vacuum for carpet. Make sure you get all the hairballs beneath the bed and dresser, too.

Now ask yourself: if you were a woman, would you want to find out how your clothes look crumpled on the floor?

If the answer is "yes," then you are good to go, sir!

DUDE

<u>Pre-Flight Checklist</u>

A pilot runs through a specific checklist prior to each flight; he does it in the same sequence, the same way every time. While you may not be a fighter jock looking to successfully pull a 9g turn before going to guns, you *are* looking to pull an overnight guest onto your jock before successfully firing your gun.

You, then, also need a pre-flight checklist.

But in this case, you are both aviator and aircraft. And everything has to be perfect prior to taxiing onto the runway.

Don't think of yourself as Maverick. You are Ice Man. You are thorough and precise. You never make a mistake. (Besides, you'd never play beach volleyball in your jeans, and Val Kilmer is, like, a million times cooler than Tom Cruise now, anyway.)

<u>Pre-Shower</u>

Weapons: Tiny scissors, tweezers, dry razor, Q-tips

Just like when cleaning the apartment, we're going to start at the top and work our way down.

___ **Eyebrows**. If you stare in the mirror and notice an uncanny resemblance to your Uncle Walter, you need to grab the scissors and start hacking away at those runaway brows.

___ **Nose hairs**. Ah, ah, ah! Not so fast. Before you start peeking into those stalactite-lined caves you call nostrils, take a close look at the top and outsides of your actual nose. Chances are you'll find some rogue hairs. Tweeze away, fella. Next, take those scissors and start chopping away inside the nostrils. Keep in mind: Ms. Right Now is probably shorter than you. This means she will have a steeper sightline into your nasal nests. Tilt your head back and take a second look from a different angle. Snip, snip. (Car owners, your rearview mirror will prove *incredibly* helpful in identifying nose hairs that need to go. Yes, seriously.)

__ **Ears**. ER doctors will tell you to never put anything smaller than your elbow into your ears. Now, with that PSA out of the way, let me tell you to arm yourself with Q-tips and go drilling like an ambidextrous coal miner. Repeat with clean swabs until the tips emerge from your ears still white. (Note: For those older than 35, you are a 2:1 shot for ear hair. Snip, snip. Sob, sob.)

__ **Neck**. Take a dry razor and lightly clean up the whiskers that have sprung up like wild flowers on the sides of your neck from your ears down to your traps (I'm giving you the benefit of the doubt that you do, in fact, have trapezius muscles). Next, run your hand over the back of your neck. Feel anything furry? Hmm, that's what a female roommate of mine called an "Ass Neck." Sounds like a deal breaker. Cleaning up this crucial area may require you to seek outside help. In a pinch, take the dry razor and lightly run it down your neck. Periodically duck into the shower and blow on the razor to unclog it; this way, no hairs hit the bathroom floor that you cleaned earlier. *You* did *clean it earlier, didn't you?!*

___ **Upper back and shoulders**. Twist your upper torso both ways to check for Backne. Women don't want to run their fingernails over your skin and rip the top off a whitehead. If you find 'em, pop 'em. Please resist the teenager within you screaming, "Hit the mirror! Hit the mirror!" You just cleaned that glass, remember? Be sure to get some soap on that open wound once you're in the shower.

___ **Big Jim and the Twins**. I don't care if you Manscape or if you don't. But she might.

___ **Rub one out**. Like the guy says in *Something About Mary*, you can't go on a date with a loaded gun in your pocket.

In Shower

___ If you didn't dry clean your shirt and you can't/won't iron, then hang it in the bathroom while you're in the shower. Crank the hot water. The steam should help with the wrinkles. And then go buy some carbon emissions credits. And, if you're a California resident, pray for your eternal soul.

___ Do *not* pee in the shower. You just spent twenty minutes scrubbing that floor! Eau de Piss is not the scent she wants to find in the bathroom. (Note: You can totally go back to peeing in the shower after she's gone.)

___ Blow your nose. Hard. Gotta clear out any hangers.

___ Aim the showerhead all over the place to make sure you wash away all the snot, dead pubes, etc.

Post-Shower

Weapons: Visine, nail clippers

__ **Eyes**. After spending hours in a haze of dust mites and cleaning solutions, your eyes probably resemble road maps. Grab some Visine and get the red out.

__ **Face**. Shavers, please be careful to not cut yourself. And be sure to even up your sideburns; you don't want one up in Atlanta and one down in Miami.

__ Beard guys, hopefully, you have already invested in a trimmer, because unless you've got the precision of a model from a Gillette shaving commercial, then you'll risk making it patchy and inconsistent. If you're usually rockin' facial hair, for the love of bearded Jesus, do not make this the night to go clean-shaven. There's a glow to a man's face after a full shave that almost looks unnatural, like seeing Mr. T with a proper haircut. Give it at least a day before you go for the complete shave. Trim before you shower, the water will wash away all the stray hairs.

___ Be sure to check the area below your Adam's Apple for wily whiskers.

___ **Fingernails**. You don't want to remind her of Wolverine, at least not when it comes to your hands. Also, clip off any hang nails or damaged cuticles. (Yes, "cuticles" is a weird word.)

___ **Toenails**. Do your toenails resemble your Dad's? Take advantage of the fact they've been softened by the shower's hot water; trim those bad boys down to a length TSA would allow on a domestic flight.

___ **Cologne**. A little is *too much*. Once, on a trip home to my parents' house, I applied a "dash" of Nautica Sport to my wrists and then rubbed my neck. My sister, sitting upstairs in the dining room, exclaimed, "Whoa!" before I'd even reached the top step. *Bon voyage, Nautica.* And, despite what the commercials claim, chicks hate Axe; they know you're only using it because you saw the guy in the commercial have a threesome at the super market. Just smell like you; she'll dig it.

Post-Dressing

___ Check to make sure you're wearing a belt. Seems silly, but lots of guys forget it – Jerry Seinfeld went two TV seasons without wearing one. Your belt should match your shoes. Regardless, whether your shirt is tucked in or not, you should be wearing a belt. If it is tucked in, please don't mix brown shoes with a black belt (or vice versa). A true fashion Nazi would tell you that your belt and shoes should be the same *shade* as well… but, hey, one problem at a time.

___ If you ignored the earlier advice on steaming your shirt, it might have annoying bumps on the shoulders from having been on the hanger a long time. These are easy to remove – without an iron! Simply wet your fingertips with water from the bathroom faucet, and pat down the bumps. Get them fairly damp. As the bumps dry out, they will vanish.

___ Set your phone to "vibrate." You don't want it beeping all through dinner, especially if it's the other woman

texting repeatedly. If you end up making out on the couch –
Atta, baby! – reset the phone to silent, so she can't feel the
vibrations through your pants pocket.

AFTERWORD

What are you doing sitting around reading this?!

Get out there, soldier, and find a Ms. Right Now to bring back to your sparkling pad!

ACKNOWLEDGMENTS

An old guy wrote this book, but fortunately he found a young guy to help him steer clear of pop culture icebergs like mentions of *The Love Boat*. (Ask your dad.)

Without Will Neal's input and humor this book would still be stuck in a file on my Mac, instead of helping dozens of his peers across the country. GO IRISH!

For the front and back covers, I had a rough concept that I thought would humorously inform potential readers of the book's content. Christine Georgiades, illustrator extraordinaire, brought that concept to life better than I had envisioned.

.

About The Author

Jamie Reidy is a University of Notre Dame graduate and a U.S. Army veteran. His first book "Hard Sell: The Evolution of a Viagra Salesman" served as the basis for the feature film *Love and Other Drugs*, starring Jake Gyllenhaal as "Jamie." Real-life Jamie really likes typing that sentence. He has published two other books, but nobody wanted to turn them into movies.

www.ingramcontent.com/pod-product-compliance
Lightning Source LLC
Chambersburg PA
CBHW060142050426
42448CB00010B/2249